A LENS BOOK

THE HUMAN BODY

Fountaindale Public Library
Bolingbrook, IL
(630) 759-2102

RP KIDS
PHILADELPHIA

CELLS

Cells are the smallest self-contained unit in the human body. They have an essential role to play in coming together to form human tissue. Tissues then come together to make organs. Our bodies are made up of billions of cells!

There are many different types of cells, but all are made up of the same three elements: membrane, which is the outer skin; cytoplasm, where all vital bodily functions take place; and the nucleus, which controls and directs these functions.

RED BLOOD CELLS

Red blood cells are also called erythrocytes. Their main job is to deliver oxygen from the lungs to the body's tissues and to carry carbon dioxide from the tissues back to the lungs. Our body produces 150 million red blood cells every day, but it also destroys just as many!

STEM CELLS

Stem cells are cells that are not fully developed; they multiply but don't have a specific job to do yet. Thus, they can turn into any type of cell. There are two types, embryonic and adult, which are needed to regenerate tissue.

DNA

DNA, or deoxyribonucleic acid, is located within the cell nucleus. It holds all the necessary instructions to determine how the cell develops and what it does. It has a double helix shape.

INDIVIDUAL DIFFERENCES

Why are some people tall and others short? Some have blond hair and others dark? Some have blue eyes and some brown?

Inherited traits, otherwise known as our gene pool, determine these physical attributes and make us all unique individuals. Genes are located in our DNA and contain all the information needed to make an individual person.

To do this, special molecules called proteins are needed. Without them, the human body wouldn't be able to develop at all. Genes are passed down to us from our parents, which explains why members of the same family often look alike!

HAIR

The hair on our head consists of piliferous outgrowths of the outer layer of the skin. Composed of solid proteins like keratin, hair can vary in color and thickness. Like everything else, these characteristics are decided by our genes.

HEIGHT

Height is the distance measured from the top of our heads to the soles of our feet. It is also decided by our genes and varies from person to person. Over time, humans have grown taller, and we are now much taller than our ancestors!

EYES

Eyes are the sense organ with specific receptors for visual stimuli. These stimuli are sent to the brain, which processes them and turns them into images. The human eye only has receptors for three colors—green, blue, and red—but it merges them so we see them all!

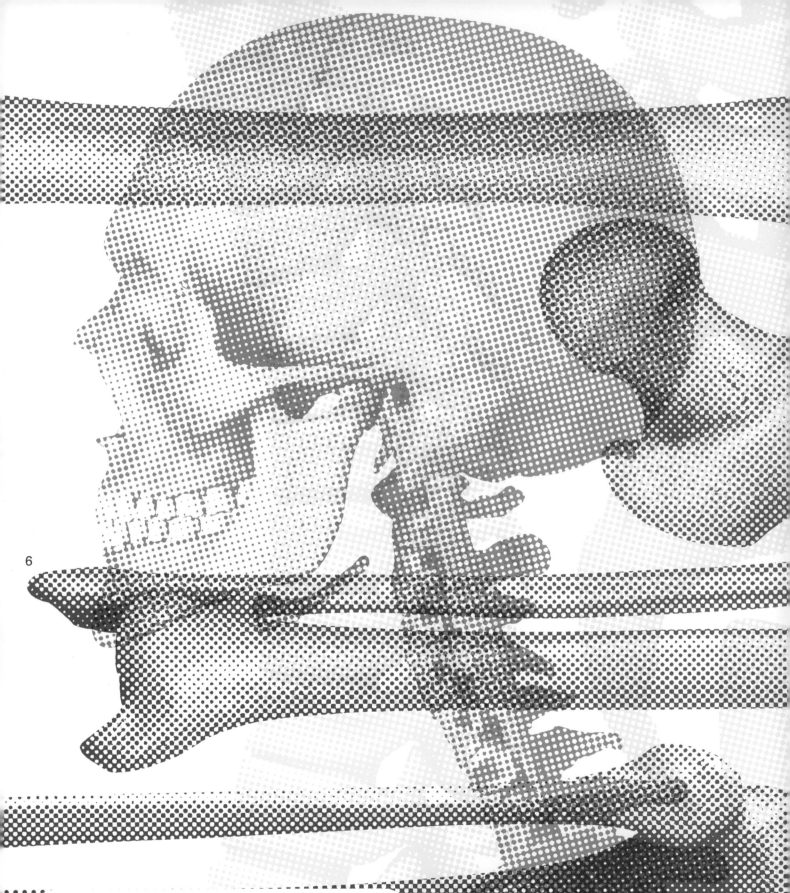

6

SKELETON

The skeleton is the framework that supports the human body; it is composed of 206 different bones and cartilage. Bones are connected to each other by around 70 joints.

The skeletal system serves many purposes: it holds us up and supports our muscles, allowing us to move, and also protects the softer, more delicate parts of the body, like the internal organs. Bones are made up of several mineral-rich layers, which makes them strong and able to withstand heavy weight. They are also split into different types depending on their shape.

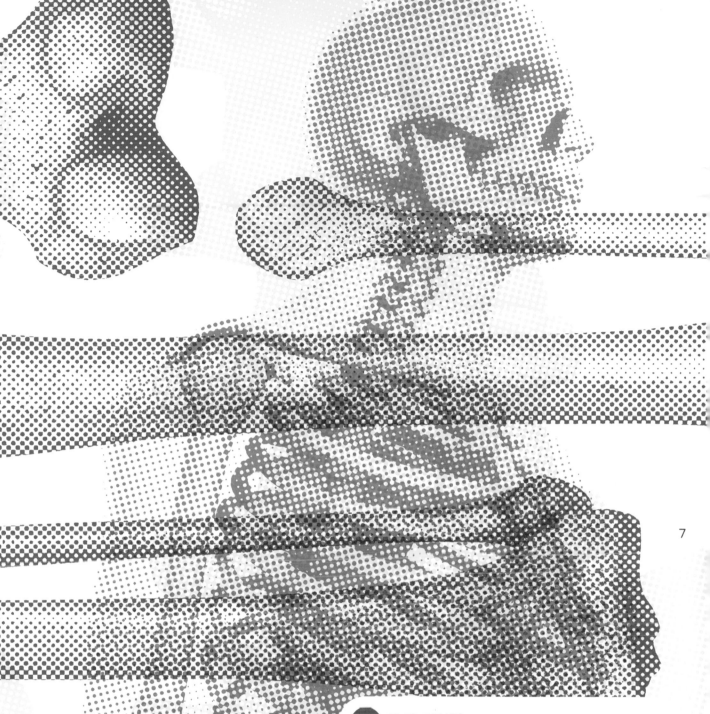

FLAT BONES

The flat bones get their name from the way they grow into broad, flat plates. This bone type includes the cranial bones (skull), the scapulae (shoulder blades), the sternum, and the hip bones.

SHORT BONES

The short bones are as long as they are wide and relatively small. They provide support and facilitate movement in the part of the body in which they are located, such as the hands and feet.

LONG BONES

The long bones make up the limbs—our arms and legs, in other words. They are elongated in shape, thinner in the middle and wider at the ends, and are connected to one another by joints.

MUSCULAR SYSTEM

Every day we move in a million different ways without giving it a thought, yet each movement is the result of a complex mechanism involving different parts of the body.

The muscular system is a system of organs—called muscles—that contract to sustain vital functions of the body and circulate substances like blood and nourishment. Together with the skeletal system, the muscular system maintains posture and enables movement.

There are thought to be about 752 muscles in the human body—but no one can agree on the exact number!

SKELETAL MUSCLES

Muscles connected to the skeleton are called skeletal muscles. They are formed of muscle fiber, are usually long and thin in shape, and they are reached by nerve endings conveying the impulses that cause muscle contraction and movement.

MUSCLE FIBER

Muscle fiber, or myocyte, is the building block of muscle tissue. It is made up of long, tapered cells, which can also shorten depending on stimuli received from nerves. Muscle fiber can be smooth or striated.

VOLUNTARY AND INVOLUNTARY MUSCLES

Muscles are split into two types: voluntary—or red, striated muscles—which we consciously choose to move, such as face muscles; and the involuntary muscles, like those of the digestive system or bronchi.

Involuntary muscles are smooth and, overseeing our vital organs, move without our conscious control.

HANDS

Hands are an essential part of the body; we need them to hold objects, to perform a variety of actions, and to interact with the world around us via the sensations we receive from the skin and our sense of touch. Moreover, hands help us to express ourselves in gestures.

10

BONES OF THE HAND

There are 27 different bones in the hand. They can be split into three broad groups: the carpals, in the wrist area; the metacarpals, connecting the wrist to the fingers; and the phalanges, which are the finger bones.

TENDONS OF THE HAND

Tendons are fibrous cords that attach muscles to bone. There are two types of tendons in the hands: the flexor and extensor tendons. Each type are connected to different types of muscle to allow the hands to open and close.

MUSCLES OF THE HAND

The hand has 19 different muscles, which can be split into extrinsic and intrinsic types. The former includes the flexor and extensor muscles, responsible for most of the movements we make with our hands. The latter are located in the palm and move the fingers.

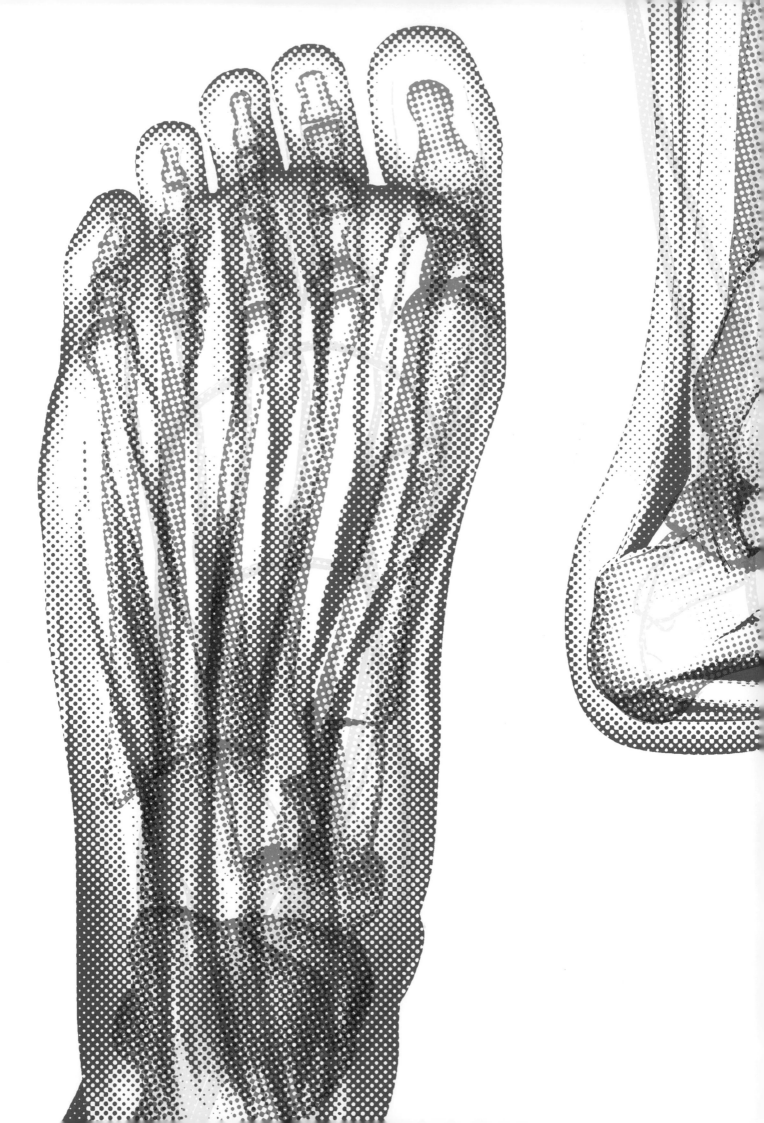

12

FEET

Our feet have a relatively complex structure, given that they need to sustain our body weight and facilitate our movements. According to some estimates, in a lifetime our feet cover the equivalent of five complete trips around the world—over 124,000 miles (200.000 km)!

 ## VEINS IN THE FEET

Our feet are crossed by a fine network of veins. One of the main ones is the great saphenous vein, also called the long saphenous vein. It begins at the front of the foot and runs up the entire length of the leg.

 ## FOOT BONES

There are 26 bones in the foot and, like the hands, they can be split into three groups: the tarsus, located in the ankle; the metatarsus, between the ankle and toes; and the phalanges.

 ## TENDONS IN THE FOOT

Like hands, our feet also have a series of tendons connecting bones to muscles. One of these is the Achilles tendon, located at the back of the foot.

SENSE OF HEARING

Hearing, namely our ability to hear and process sounds, is one of the five senses. It is the first one to develop.

EAR CANAL

The ear canal extends from the pinna and is considered part of the outer ear, joining it to other more internal parts of the system and functioning like a passageway.

EARDRUM

The eardrum is a fine membrane with the delicate function of protecting the tiny, innermost parts of the auditory system. It transmits sound waves to them, which they then convey to the brain.

HEARING

Our auditory system is particularly complex, extending deep inside the cranium. It also has an external, or peripheral, portion, which is visible from the outside. Our ears are, in other words, part of the system, and the pinna have the function of "gathering" sounds and conveying them to the inner part of the system.

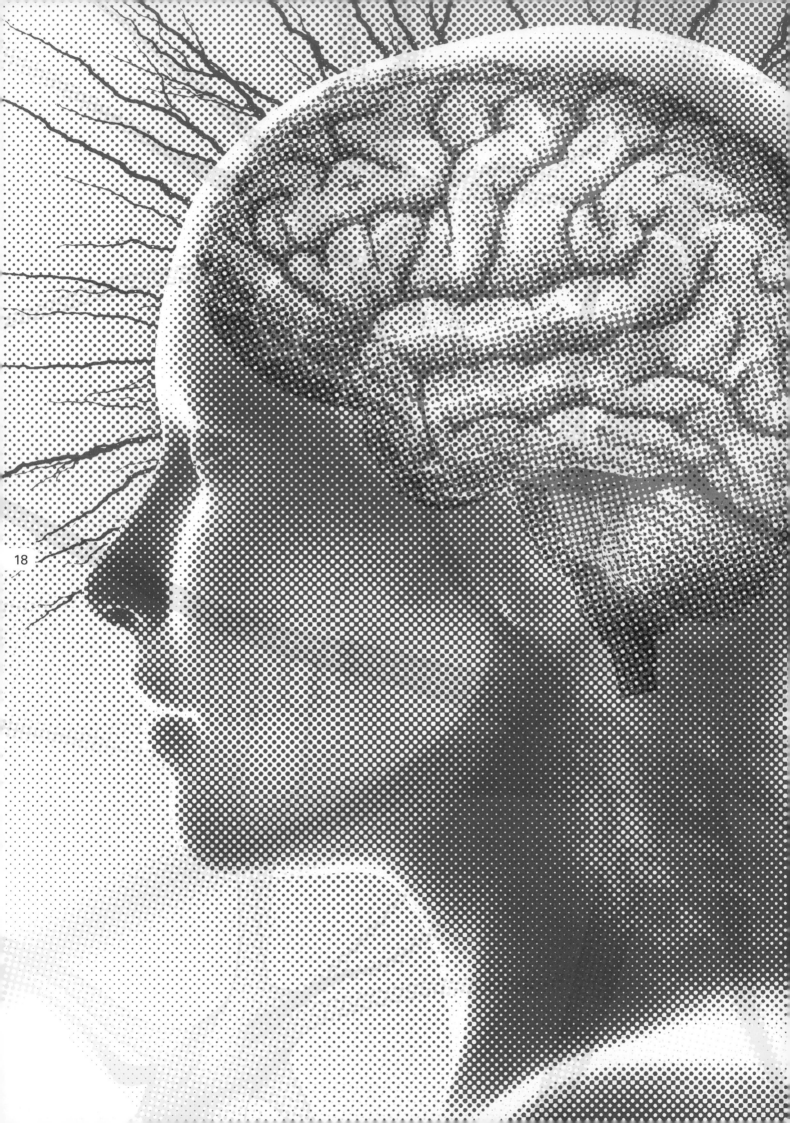

BRAIN

Contained within the cranial cavity, the brain is one of the biggest, heaviest, and most complex organs in the human body. Take, for example, the many functions it performs: controlling vital functions like heartbeat and breathing; processing stimuli received from the five senses; controlling movement, language, memory, and emotions. It is the ultimate operating system and an object of ongoing study.

BRAIN AND LITTLE BRAIN

The brain has two hemispheres, right and left, joined by the corpus callosum. It also has four parts called lobes. In the lower part of the brain stem is the cerebellum (little brain), which controls balance and movement.

NEURONS

Neurons are the basic unit of nerve cells in the brain, which can have 10 to 100 billion of them!

SYNAPSES

Synapses are structures that connect neurons, transmitting electrical or chemical signals from one cell to another. Neurons can have anywhere from 5,000 to 100,000 synapses!

DIGESTIVE SYSTEM

The digestive system consists of a group of hollow organs, comprising the pharynx, esophagus, stomach, and intestine, which work together to break down, move through the body, and ultimately expel the food that we eat. Moreover, the system is connected to glands like the liver, gall bladder, and pancreas.

THE START OF DIGESTION

Numerous glands are involved in the digestive process and each has a different function; the liver, which helps to turn food into useful substances; and the pancreas, which produces digestive juices to aid in the absorption of nutrients.

INTESTINE

The intestine is shaped like a long, coiled tube and comprises the small intestine and the large intestine (also called the colon). It is 26 feet (8 m) long in total.

VILLI

Once food has gone through the stomach, it travels to the small intestine, which is 23 feet (7 m) long. The membrane of the small intestine is lined with villi, small projections that absorb nutrients in the food we eat. The food then passes into the large intestine, where the digestive process is completed.

21

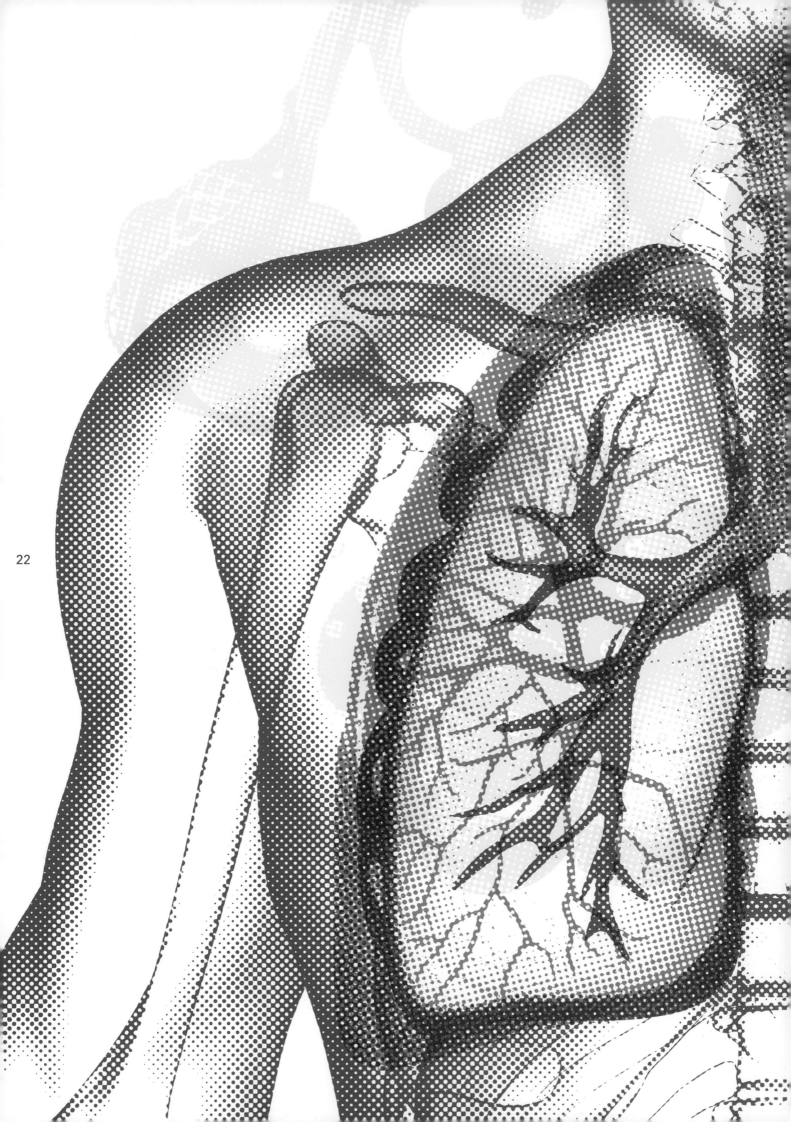

RESPIRATORY SYSTEM

Working in close connection with the circulatory system, the respiratory system enables us to take in oxygen and expel carbon dioxide. It is formed by the nose, larynx, pharynx, trachea, lungs, and bronchi.

LUNGS

The human body has two lungs, situated within the ribcage and separated from each other. They are covered by a thin layer of tissue called the pleura, which is essential to the role of the lungs in removing carbon dioxide from the blood and replacing it with oxygen.

BRONCHI

The human body has two bronchi, a right one and a left one, which branch into many smaller tubes called bronchioles and alveoli. Their job is to carry air from the trachea to the lungs.

ALVEOLI

The alveoli are the terminal ends of the bronchi. Despite being small, the tiny cavities have an important role to play: they enable the exchange of respiratory gases between the blood and the atmosphere. The lungs couldn't work without the alveoli!

CARDIOVASCULAR SYSTEM

The cardiovascular system regulates circulation of the blood and comprises three main parts: blood vessels, blood, and the heart. The heartbeat regulates blood flow and keeps it constantly circulating.

The heart is a striated but involuntary muscle. It contracts autonomously and functions like a pump, pushing the one-and-a-half gallons (five liters) of blood we have around our bodies.

24

HEART

The heart is a striated, hollow, muscular organ divided into four chambers: two atria—one right and one left—in the upper part, and two ventricles in the lower part—again one right and one left.

VEINS

Veins have the job of carrying blood from all parts of the body back to the heart. The blood that's transported typically contains waste products.

OXYGEN EXCHANGE

The heart directs every aspect of blood flow. The lungs and heart, for example, are connected by the pulmonary veins, which regulate the exchange between oxygen-rich blood and blood containing carbon dioxide.

THE MIRACLE OF LIFE

The development of a new life is a fascinating process lasting nine months and comprising many delicate and complex stages. We all start life as a single cell. This cell multiplies to create tissues, which then combine into organs until a new human being forms and is ready to be born.

FERTILIZATION

Fertilization takes place when the male reproductive cell—sperm—penetrates the female one, called an ovum. The result of this union is the zygote, the single cell from which life begins.

CELL DEVELOPMENT

The zygote is the cell from which a baby grows; in twenty-four hours, it splits into two cells, then into four, and so on. Two weeks after fertilization, the cells form the embryo, and from the third month of gestation, the embryo becomes the fetus.

GESTATION

Human gestation, or pregnancy, normally lasts 37 weeks, although the exact term can vary. It is typically split into three-month periods, each marked by specific stages of development of the fetus.

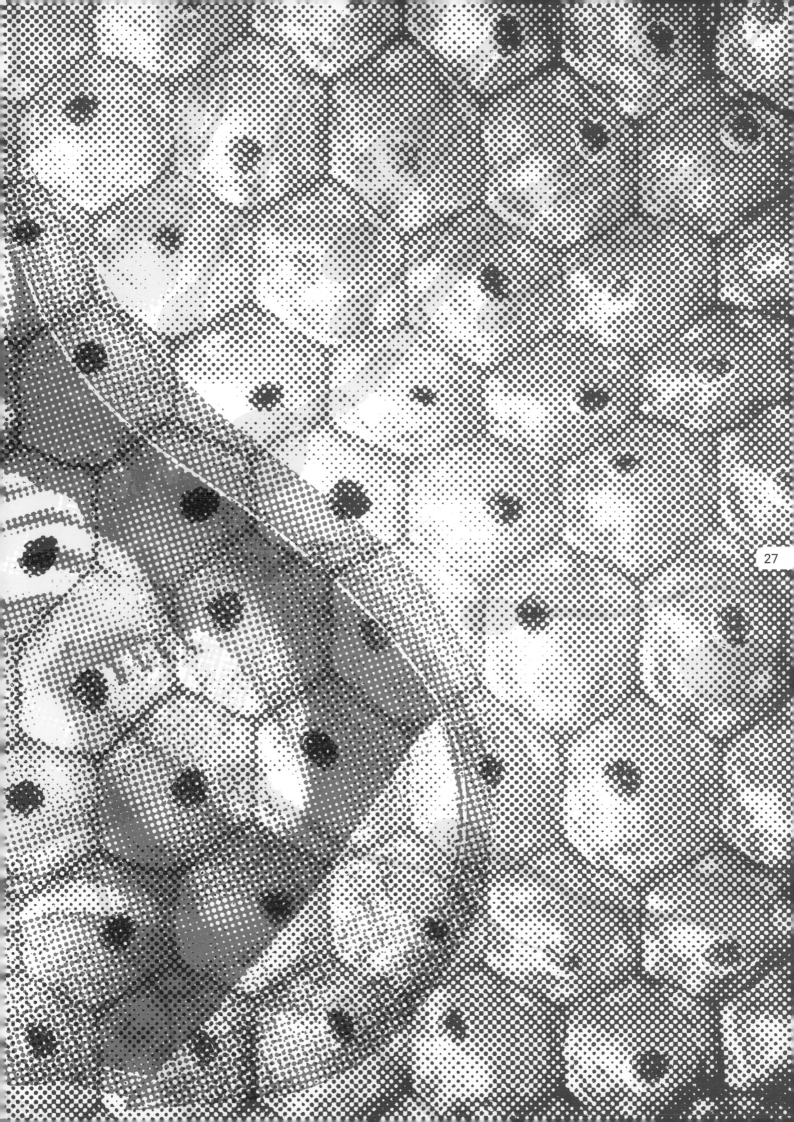

Copyright © 2017 by Sassi Editore SRL

Hachette Book Group supports the right to free expression and the
value of copyright. The purpose of copyright is to encourage writers
and artists to produce the creative works that enrich our culture.

The scanning, uploading, and distribution of this book without
permission is a theft of the author's intellectual property. If you would
like permission to use material from the book (other than for review
purposes), please contact permissions@hbgusa.com. Thank you for
your support of the author's rights.

Running Press Kids
Hachette Book Group
1290 Avenue of the Americas, New York, NY 10104
www.runningpress.com/rpkids
@RP_Kids

Printed in China

Originally published in 2017 by Sassi Editore SRL in Italy
First U.S. Edition: May 2018

Published by Running Press Kids, an imprint of Perseus Books, LLC,
a subsidiary of Hachette Book Group, Inc. The Running Press Kids
name and logo is a trademark of the Hachette Book Group.

The Hachette Speakers Bureau provides a wide range of authors
for speaking events. To find out more, go to
www.hachettespeakersbureau.com or call (866) 376-6591.

The publisher is not responsible for websites (or their content)
that are not owned by the publisher.

Images © Shutterstock

Library of Congress Control Number: 2017958094

ISBN: 978-0-7624-9224-4 (hardcover)

LEO

10 9 8 7 6 5 4 3 2 1